NOT IN MY OWN STRENGTH

With God All Things Are Possible

Charlotte Patterson

NOT IN MY OWN STRENGTH
With God All Things Are Possible

ISBN (Paperback): 978-1-964494-71-5
ISBN (Ebook): 978-1-964494-72-2

PROMINENT
BOOKS
EDGE

5830 E 2nd St, Ste 7000 #9983
Casper, WY 82609
USA

CONTENTS

INTRODUCTION

Pain has a remedy. Some will take the natural medication. I took Jesus—the TRUTH, the written WORD OF GOD. It brings results as you apply it as you take action to resolve the issues in your life. I found out a lot of things about myself while writing. It was not all good. When we finally discover the things in our lives that are not good, that's the time to take action. I could not take action; my pain put scars in my heart. I held on to the pain for years. I can gladly say that part soon passed, and then it was time for healing. Healing was a process for me. Deep scarring takes time to heal, and many layers must be pulled off. Many deliverances took place in my life as I was going through what I had to face. There was a possibility of divorce, there was a possibility of Restoration; I chose to have God restore. In order to be restored, there are many things you will have to come face to face within your personal life. You will say, "Oh, I didn't know that you were going through such a trial in your life with your family." Plan to spend much more time with God than you already do. You will find victory in your story.

NOT IN MY OWN
STRENGTH

I have known Billy all my life, even without realizing who he was. We were in the first grade together. I remembered this young boy later when talking to him because he sat behind me and pulled on my two long pigtails. When we were growing up, we lived and played in the same neighborhood and were in a different apartment complex across the yard from each other. Since he was from a military family, Billy moved away from our hometown at a young age. During this time, he would come back home to visit his relatives off and on. During these visits, he would ask his cousin where I was and what I was doing.

As the years passed, his mom had fallen ill, so they decided to move back to Oklahoma. It was the beginning of a relationship, and I did not know where it would lead. When Billy's mom passed, it was a sad time for him, but it put us both in a good place in our lives going into the future. Looking back at it from today, I knew God was in control. Everything that I was feeling about him, I knew it had to have come from the Holy Spirit.

Growing up, we knew about God because we were a part of a Baptist church, where the traditions of men were being taught with the Bible, which is still being taught today to some. Since they spoke in tongues, I don't remember ever encountering speaking in tongues because only my grandma would speak in tongues that I had heard from the church. I learned later that the Holy Spirit was helping me.

When I was in a relationship with my oldest daughter's father, she was one and a half, and we lived in her father's apartment. You know how the old folk call it "shacking"? I agree, that's what it was. During this time, I would see a strange blue car parked outside of the apartment. I didn't recognize the car until I saw it around where we would be hanging out sometimes. It turns out that Billy would sit outside of the apartment as though he were waiting for me. However, he was, instead, just sitting in front of our apartment. At that time, I had no idea what he was thinking; Now, I suppose he was thinking about me during that year of 1987 when he was out there.

A father provides for their child, gives them attention, gives them council, cries with them, takes them up in his arms, and holds them until the tears are gone. To run and play is a joy to both the parent and child. You, as a parent, participate in their long-life activities as they grow up. As a parent, you help them make into reality the dreams and goals they have. Then, before you know it, they are getting married. I am grateful that my daughter found a father in my now husband, Billy. To the women who get married, you cannot allow the pride or ego of the man you married to stop you from letting your child have contact with him or receive child support if the other parent wants to be involved with the child. There should be a discussion and an agreement with what you both decide. Men do not let your ego or pride make decisions for you that would end up in a not so good conversation. Pride is not of God, and your ego is attached to your flesh. Move yourself out of the way and let the wisdom of God speak to your heart on how the both of you should deal with the situation.

Whether it's a boy or a girl, it's healthy to let the biological father participate in the child's life. If they don't want to participate in the child's life, then that is something different. So, men, you do more harm than good because it's not about you are being able to take care of your new family or you are being the better man. It is about the child. So, sit with and talk with the child, then ask the child questions about what it is they are feeling consider their input on the new relationship now that their mom is married to someone else. This goes for women as well because women can abandon their children too.

Just know that you don't have to be a counselor to speak to any child because all you need is wisdom. In Proverbs 22:6, it says, "Train up a child in the way he should go: and when he is old, he will not depart from it." This is talking about training your child in the Word of the Lord. It means to teach them the speech of God, not yours alone. Don't be compelled to rewrite the words given to us to train your children too, for they will continue to need counsel from us as their life progresses, and we should still be able to feed the Word to them as they grow older.

We have many stages that we go through as we grow up to become young men and women; therefore, we should not only count on our parents but the Word of God for examples on how to live. You are our letter (of recommendation) written in our hearts, recognized and ready to everyone. You show that you are a letter from Christ, delivered by us, written not with ink but with the Spirit of the living God, not on tablets of stone but on tablets of human hearts. From this, we know that we are the newsletters read by our children on this Earth. So, do not let society dictate how you raise your children because you have the instruction guide called the Bible.

By the grace of our Lord, Jesus Christ, some of our children are drawn to Christ by the prayers of the righteous. We cover them in everything they do, in every part of their life, until the will of God is bringing forth fruit in them. The purpose in them manifests. James 5:16b says, "The effectual fervent prayers of a righteous man availed much." When she was on this Earth, my grandmother prayed fervently; she was righteous. Her fervent prayers have followed the generations of my family. They are still activating in the spirit realm. This is what I carry in my spirit to remind me of the days and nights of her praying. She carried our family. We as adults leave children out of conversations that we think are for adults only, especially when it pertains to them. We cannot think that our children cannot handle a conversation. Coming down to their level is part of the communication package we should be able to do. If you do not know how to talk to your child on their level or talk to them at all, you need help yourself. Communication is key, and I am still learning how to communicate with the adult children I have now. You will have to grow as an adult, while at the same time, they are growing as the child while becoming the adult. However, do not speak to them as though they are an adult.

Without a godly-structured family, single parents will have a hard time parenting alone. So, God must be first. It is also important to remember that our children are priority after our spouses, not before. However, that does not mean you love your children any less. There is just an order to a family structure, even if you are not married. In Colossians 3:18–21, it states:

> Ephesians 5:22–25 Wives, be subject to your hus-
> bands (out of respect for their position as protec-
> tor, and their accountability to God), as is proper
> and fitting in the Lord. Husbands, love your wives
> (with an affectionate, sympathetic, selfless love
> that always seeks the best for them) and do not
> be embittered or resentful toward them (because
> of the responsibilities of marriage). Ephesians 6:1
> Children, obey your parents (as God's representa-
> tives) in all things, for this (attitude of respect and
> obedience) is well pleasing to the Lord (and will
> bring you God's promised blessings). Ephesians
> 6:4 Fathers, do not provoke or irritate or exasper-
> ate your children (with demands that are trivial
> or unreasonable or humiliating or abusive; nor
> by favoritism or indifference; treat them tenderly
> with loving-kindness), so they will not lose heart
> and become discouraged or unmotivated (with
> their spirits broken).

This means that God must *always* be put first. In the beginning, my intentions were not to have any children until I was married. If I had made this vow to the Lord, then I would have kept it better. However, this was only a vow made to myself, not to God, and I let someone talk me into having sex before it was time. During this time, my daughter's father talked to me about marriage; he even talked about getting me a ring, but he never went through with it. By the time I decided to leave him, the baby was already born. After my daughter's birth, we were together for four years total, the only thing that I regret about it was that I spent too much of my time talking to myself. I kept promising myself that I was going to do this and that, but they all ended up being false promises made to myself. At the time, I was eighteen. I learned later that just because a guy talks to you about marriage, it does not mean he is going to marry you. So, until he gives you a ring, do not trust the words he speaks. Men speak swelling words to get what they want, and sometimes, they get it. Don't be fooled; don't fall into this trap. All kinds of conversations are being spoken out there today, but if you are a godly woman or a godly man, you would want to do the right thing, going about it in the right way. Do not rush your relationships. Remember, God is the Author! God Bless You.

Ladies, you are not a man's dirty laundry, so do not act like you are, you do not have a return policy tagged on your sleeve. Women are disrespected in these days and times because the women of today do not seem as if they know who they are. Women down-grade themselves, letting men call them out of their name and treat them like trash. This is not respect, it is mental abuse. It affects the mind and the future of who you are. It's not how God intended you to live. Women have become enslaved by their own relationship, and they don't even know it. If I had listened to my mother, I would have had a record of divorce. I love my mother, but sometimes, mothers are not right. We surely are not right about everything. If we are alive, we are here to help and assist. Thankfully, the Holy Spirit was in control and made it so that I knew that there was no way I was going to stay with him just because I had a child by him. I would have been miserable if I did. I liked peace so much that I would walk away from someone to get it. At one point in my life, when I was with my daughter's father, I thought he was the one because he talked about moving out of state. I thought he was the one I would be traveling with. This is because my steps were ordered by the Lord. He told me when I was fifteen years old that I would be married to someone who traveled the world. Little did I know it would be Billy. These words spoken to me by God would stick with me for the rest of my life.

Growing up, my mom was a single mother with six children. She did her best to do a good job of raising us, my mom taught my siblings and myself what to do and what not to do; that if we ever had children, to not be fooled because they are always watching your every move. After all, they learn from their parents more than many realize. Aside from my mother, my precious grandmother taught me so much. When I was with her, she took me to church with her, and my mom would make sure that I was ready every time to go with her.

I was second to the oldest among my siblings. When my mom had to work, I was put in charge of the house in her stead. I had to make sure everything was done, and everyone had to do their part. I had to make sure it would all be done by the time my mom got home from work. If it didn't get done, then I would be the one my mom woke up in middle of the night, sometimes at two in the morning, to do what should have been done earlier that day. While I looked after the house, my older sister was in college. During this time, I ended up resenting my mom for making me stay home instead of letting me participate in any activities. Since my mom made sure I did everything needed to run the house, I practically had no childhood. I became mature at a very young age and had to grow up quickly. For a long time, I held all this against my mom because it was not easy being responsible for everyone while she was at work since I was not her and I was very young. However, what I did to take care of my siblings and my mom's house, I ended up doing the same for my own household. All that I had learned, I ended up putting to work with my own family, and it certainly paid off years later. Currently, I'm married with five children, and I've realized that I have done the same to my daughter; at least, it's like what I experienced anyway.

Often, as parents, we say that we didn't have a choice but to leave the oldest in charge when we were busy. Even now, I don't have an answer for that nor a solution since parents tend to look toward the oldest to help out when they need it. Thankfully, I did not go as far as my mom because I was married. I can count on the one hand how many times she stayed with her brother and sisters. We did not treat her as though her time did not matter to us, like how I felt with my mom. It took me many years to release myself from the resentment and to forgive her because the hurt was still present. In the year 2022, I finally got my release; I forgave her. I don't think I ever told her how I felt. I'm going to make sure I tell her.

KNOWING MY DAD,
WHO BECAME MY FATHER,
ON HIS DEATH BED

Learning who your father is at a young age, it was a satisfying moment because I found out who he was; it was a disappointing moment because he had done nothing for me, knowing that I had been around for years. After seeing this man's face around town and not knowing he was my dad, I had mixed feelings about what was going on. This was bittersweet. My mom begin to tell me the story about them. My dad, I believe, was a good person in general, his history with women was not good. When my mom told me the story of how he refused to claim me as his daughter, I was about 13 years old. At the time, she explained to me that there was no interest in me on his part. As I got older, my mind was more mature, I could understand more clearly what my mom was saying to me, and that was, he did not want to be a part of my life. There were no harsh feelings of unforgiveness toward him. In my mind, I just wanted to get to know my father and who he was. I had nothing against him. As a matter of fact, I didn't even ask any questions. I started to spend time with him. I would spend the night over at his house, and we would have dinner together. I was shy, so I didn't talk much at all. I began to get to know him. Growing up, I had seen a picture of my grandmother on my father's side, and I was lucky to know most of my relatives on my father's side, I had two brothers and one sister. For some reason, my sister did not like me. I was thirteen years old when I found out that she even existed. Anyway, life went on for me because, for those who know me, I am a no-nonsense kind of person. I love, care for, and can get along with anyone. However, I do mind my own business and do not mess with anyone.

One day, out of the blue, I got a text from my sister. I was in shock and ran to my husband.

"Look! I got a text from my sister!"

"What?" he asked.

I said, "I got a text from my sister; you know, the one that was not talking to me."

In response, he said to me, "Open door." Yes, it was an open door, and it was so wide open. At first, I did not answer for a couple of days since I was still in shock. Then, I finally texted back. If I remember correctly, she had talked to our brother.

He said to her, "She's probably in shock from you texting her after all these years."

I laughed because it was true, I was stunned, and I had no words. She was like our dad more than any one of us. She talked like him, her voice was loud and heavy, and she definitely looked like him. I only know two of my siblings on my father's side of the family, and I have never met nor seen any other siblings besides the two. I probably will never meet them, and I'll never have any ill feelings toward my dad's side of the family because he left me. I pray that they will live a full and healthy life and that the grace and mercy of God shine down on them. Growing up as a little girl without a father, growing up to be a grown woman, I say" I am not alone.

I did not know my father until I was thirteen years old. During that time, I remember my father coming to pick me up, and we would go out to eat. I would meet his friends, and they would say that I was a cutie. However, I did not know what that meant. I had an idea that he was talking about me to his friends. Even though I never asked him for anything in my life, I do remember that he gave me eighty dollars when I was twenty years old. Then some years after I got married, I was in Hawaii with my family when I got a call that he was sick. No one told me he was dying. During that period, we only spoke twice. I called him, and at the end of the first conversation, I asked him if we could spend more time together. When he agreed, I told him that he could be more of a father to me by treating me like how a father treats his daughter before we hung up. The second time I thought about talking to him, I had a sick feeling in my stomach, so I did not wait to call him. He did not answer. Instead, one of his close buddies did and told me that my father had passed away.

Even though he'd died, I still had gotten my father and daughter moment. This happened through his way of telling me that he loved me and that he was going to spend more time with me, even though he knew he was dying. I was mature enough to understand what he had said. I will never forget that moment. I was told later that he'd accepted Jesus on his death bed. I was happy because as long as he was with Jesus, I would get to see him again, and we would be able to get that father and daughter time together.

⚓

TRUTH OF BEING
A PARENT

I n the times we live in today, there are more and more single parents. There are single fathers out there, along with single mothers. My heart goes out to single mothers and fathers, but what concerns me most is the child. No single parent can fully parent a child because a father has what his son needs, and a father should hold the image of what a husband looks like for his daughter. Meanwhile, a mother has what a daughter needs and should hold the image of what a mother and wife should look like for her son. It is selfish to think of yourself back in your single stage of life. In fact, you should not look as though you are single; it should be you and God, plain and simple. This is because the picture should be God first. Once you fall in love with God, you will fall in love with your husband or wife, and they will come forth or manifest. As Genesis 2:7, "And the Lord God formed man of the dust of the ground and breathed into his nostrils the breath of life; and man became a living soul. He breathed the breath of life into the man's nostrils, and the man became a living person." Then in Genesis 21–23

> And the Lord God caused a deep sleep to fall upon Adam, and he slept: and he took one of his ribs and closed up the flesh instead thereof; And the rib, which the Lord God had taken from man, made he a woman, and brought her unto the man. And Adam said, this is now bone of my bones, and flesh of my flesh: she shall be called Woman, because she was taken out of Man.

Here, I am speaking of a woman and a man, not the same sex. This is because they are ones that can never create human life; they can only adopt. The family in which some people believe in is out of order because this does not bring a stability to the home; it only brings disfunction. Please remember that God loves everyone, and as do I. In John 3:16, it says, "For God so loved the world, that he gave his only begotten Son, that whosoever believeth in him shall not perish, but have everlasting life." Then in Romans 2:11, it says, "For there is no respect of persons with God. There is no partiality with God." To follow, in Proverbs 14:12, it says, "There is a way which seemed right unto man, but the end thereof are the ways of death." In the New International Version, it says that there is a way that appears to be right, but in the end, it leads to death. He hates the act of sin in which people think it is the correct way to live.

So, please take this opportunity to teach and educate your children on why there is only one parent in the home and be truthful; do not lie to them, and do not compromise and manip-ulate the truth. After all, you can change their way of thinking. To the mothers who have boyfriends living in your home or spending the night for a tangle, do not have your child call him "Dad" or "Uncle." You are not married, and if he is an uncle, then you're committing incest. You cannot tag a name to someone that is not related to **truth**. This is because you believe what you receive! A big example for this is when you make up a name for your child, and it really does not make any sense in the English language or any other language; as a matter of fact, you have no idea what it means, like when you decide to name your child after a fictional character in a book. Then it just so happens that the name you chose means "to lay on your back." I'm sure you can see where I am going with this. A person, or child in this case, becomes what their name means because there is a lot to a name. This is why I was incredibly careful when I named my children. It is possible that your child may become promiscuous, laying on their back, because you chose to name them a fictional character out of a book. Now they are living out what you named them.

This is true; if you know who you are, then you will become who God purposed you to be. My second oldest child gave me a long and hard labor in giving birth to her. When I woke up, I was in my room, she had a name that I had not given her, and I did not bother to change it. The first part of her name was Tre`, sounds like a boy's name. I did not think about that at the time. Later in life, she was in a relationship with a young man that was living in another state. Before she left to go visit him, I talked to her about having sex because she was a virgin. She did not listen, and he got married a year and a half later. However, this man did not want anything from her but her virginity. She was hurt by this situation and, even now, still has not healed from the pain. Later, she was introduced to the idea of having a relationship with other females by another female. This was an open door for the Enemy to come in because she never had dealt with the pain in her heart, for it was still too painful for her. Since she hasn't confronted her pain, she will not heal. When she told us, her father and I, that she did not like boys anymore, we were broken. It was not like we did not already know.

So, think about what you name your child. I pray, decree, and declare that the words of the Lord are over my daughter's life. I know who she is and who she is to become. I know that her purpose must come forth and that this is but a hick-up. It does not matter what her friends say, what they see, or what people hear. I could care less what anyone thinks about her because God has spoken, and **it shall be!**

HERE HE COMES (MY HUSBAND BILLY)

At the beginning, I did not know he was my husband. I am a strong woman, who bounces back every time, and when she does, she bounces back in control, not out of control. I just wish I had confidence at that time in who I really was through God's purpose for my life. When Billy came to town, he would always ask where I was or what I was up to. We started dating after I had graduated my senior year of high school because I had to go back for a semester to get my high school diploma since I did not get it originally because I had my oldest daughter. Before we got together, I ended my relationship with my oldest daughter's dad. When I worked at Pizza Hut, Billy would sometimes ask if I needed a ride home, or he would just sit in the parking lot while I was working and waiting. He would also see me walking to different places because I didn't have a car.

I remember this one time, before prom, he had asked a girl to the dance before he asked me. He did not let her know this, and he did not cancel their prom date either. That night, he came to pick me up, and we had a full night. However, we did run into the girl he asked originally, and my goodness, she let him have it. It was not pleasant, and he just looked at her and asked, "Are you finished?"

Then he walked away. She did not hit him or anything, but you know, when they say if words could kill, he would have been dead. At the time, I hated to see this, but he was already over it because he had who he really wanted to be with that night. Later, there was a rumor he heard that when he was going to take her to a restaurant, she said she was going to order a lot of food on the menu and that she was going to mistreat the occasion. So, I guess, after hearing that, he decided to do what he did. Of course, It didn't make it right. After being with him for about three months, he asked me to marry him. I just looked at him and did not say a thing at first; it was funny though. After six months passed, we were having a conversation, and I reminded him about what he had asked me before. I asked him to ask me again. He was confused at first, but then I repeated myself, and he did. This time, I said yes, and he put the ring on my finger. I still have it even now. It was two days after October 28, 1988 we were married, we had to go to our first Army military base: Ft. Hood in Killeen, Texas.

⚓

KILLEEN, TEXAS

We had no idea what was in store for us in Killeen, Texas, because we were a young couple just starting life together. We had no transportation, no credit, no anything. We had not planned this; as a matter of fact, we had not planned anything. Our life seemed like it was just being played out as we lived through it. At the time, we did not know anything about living for God and believing in the Son, Jesus Christ. We did know of God and of Jesus Christ, but we knew nothing about how to apply what we knew to our lives. Due to this, we could only do what we knew. When we moved, I was pregnant, and I had our baby girl shortly after getting there, about two months later.

One night, I had to go to the hospital because I was in a lot of pain. We were there for so long that it had become the wee hours of the morning. Since Billy had an inspection that morning, he left and took our baby girl with him. When he came back to the hospital, she was crying and would not stop. He asked me why she was crying because he had changed her and given her a bath. So, I asked him to give her to me. When I took off her onesie, I saw both of her feet were wet, so I called the doctor into the room. It turned out that our baby girl had second to third degree burns. After that night in the emergency room, we did not get to see our little girl. The staff took her to the burn unit in San Antonio, Texas and the doctor that took her out of the room called social services. I asked where she was, but they would not tell me. In fact, it was months before they told me anything. My heart was broken. I do not think we ever slept that day, and days went by, and we had no idea what was coming next.

Later, Billy was arrested and taken to jail. We had even made the news; it was in the Oklahoma Newspaper; it was even in the Enid Newspaper, where we were from. During this time, we were under investigation, and they went through every room. Our life, as it was, was now under a microscope. I was in shock from all the drama around me. There was a sentence put on the table very quickly, and I was told by social services to take my oldest daughter to my mom's house in Oklahoma. She could not be in the house with me while the investigation was going on. My mind then went blank, and I had no words for the situation. The one thing I did know, however, was that my hope and faith in God would not fail me. Since my spirit began to cry out, I was not worried or even bothered.

We were not troubled teens nor had a troubled childhood. Everyone does have their issues, and I am not saying we were the perfect couple, but we were young; still in our early twenties, and we were learning as we went. We stayed to ourselves. Billy was an extremely social person while I was an introvert.

At this time, if there were specific prayers to pray, I really did not know the words to them, so I prayed what was in my heart and how I felt at the time. God knew what was happening. It's not like He did not see what was going on. I even felt that

He wanted me to talk to Him. So, when I did pray, Jesus heard me. I did not know how to do anything else. I was alone since my husband was incarcerated. It would be about thirty days until I saw him again. He had tears in his eyes and a confused look on his face when he did see me again. It was easy to tell that he had never been in jail. That day, I sat and talked with him, even though I really did not know what to say. He told me that he was afraid and worried that I would have to go to prison too. In response, I told him that everything would be ok.

Later, I went to one of the highest paid lawyers in Belton County, Texas, to talk too. He said he was familiar with Billy's case because it was in the Killeen, Texas, paper. He spoke to me from a lawyer's point of view, which was not what I needed to hear. You can tell the manner of someone's thinking by the words that come out of their mouth; you know if they are living by faith or by sight, if their flesh is leading their decision making, or if they consult the Holy Spirit, if they are a believer or religious. Everything he was telling me could happen, but for me, it was not going to happen. I did not care about what anyone thought or was thinking. When I got on my knees to pray, the hand of the Lord touched me on my left shoulder. He told me that everything was going to be alright. When I heard that, I looked back over my shoulder as though someone was there. In that moment, I was not worried about anything. I knew Billy was coming home.

In the meantime, I was traveling back and forth from Killeen to Oklahoma by bus to see my daughter, KaTilla. Since I was by myself, my cousin came and stayed with me for a little while. His unit in the military would also come to check up on me. I had to hold on to the impossible. I was alone, but now, I did not feel so anymore. I knew that God was with me and that He was going to walk with me through this until it was finished. So, I developed a daily routine to keep my mind busy. Then, a few days later, I heard a knock at the door, and there Billy was, standing in front of me, just as God had shown me. It was later in the evening, and the sun was going down. What *did* blow my mind about that day was that everything was just as God had shown me.

When God speaks to you and shows you things, you must take His word by faith, for we walk by faith, not by sight (2 Cor. 5:7). Although I was happy to have Billy back, it was not over. My family was still scattered all over the place. My two-year-old was in Oklahoma with my mom, while my newborn was in foster care custody. Then, a couple of days later, we got a letter in the mail telling us where our daughter was and that we could see her. Even though months had gone by, we had not forgotten about her. I just had to focus on one situation at a time. God had to get Billy home first because he belonged with his family.

At first, we were only allowed to see our baby girl with supervised visits in the hospital in San Antonio. I would go back and forth to Brooke Army Medical Center. Then they moved her from the hospital into foster care. While the investigation was going on, Billy was allowed to work. Our time was spent like this until my newborn was about eight months old. What shall we then say to these things? If God be for us, who can be against us (Rom. 8:31)? God was always on our side. The scary part for Billy was the way that the prison system was set up because it was terrible for families. The prisons were not really concerned with rehabilitating a Black family man or Black men in general. They would just say, "Let us just put them away because they will be back anyway if we let them go."

This was not my concern, however, because I knew that Billy would not go to prison. Only God could prepare a way such as this. When it was time to go to court, I heard people say it would be difficult because what you are preparing for is the outcome. That day, we sat there in the court room with our close family. The judge put four people on the stand, including myself. This was tough for me to swallow because sitting in the court room with the judge and prosecutor was scary since we did not know the ending. All we could do was depend on the words from God that we'd hear in our ears. After a little while, the judge left the room after hearing everything to deliberate. When he did come back, he took his seat and paused. Then he took a deep breath and said, "I don't know why I am saying this, but I see two young people trying to take care of their children."

He ruled the incident an accident, and Billy was placed on parole after being fined $10,000 dollars and spending thirty days in jail. Thankfully, he was allowed to keep his military career while serving probation and thirty-day sentence only on the weekends. Because he was in the military, Billy had to report where we were going if we were to leave the state of Texas or to leave the country.

I thank my God. God got us through all of this. When you have a purpose set before you, then there is nothing that can get in the way of God carrying out His purpose for your life. You must remember that when you make certain decisions for your life, it is easier to choose God's way instead of your own if you have knowledge of knowing you have purpose. So, serve the Lord. Wait on the Lord and be of good courage, and He shall strengthen your heart. Wait, I say, on the Lord (Ps. 27:14)! This was the perfect example of walking by faith, not by sight (2 Cor.

5:7). I took this scripture to be an instruction for me. We were able to go and get our girls and rebuild our home. All praise goes to God. No one can get the credit for any word or anything that took place.

⚓

GERMANY

Babenhausen, Germany, was the next military base we were stationed at. I must tell you; I did not want to go. It was too far away from home, and it was foreign from what I knew. They spoke English but not much and not often. I was ok after being there for a little while though. During this time, we lived in a little place called Aschaffenburg. Our landlord lived above us, and a Turkish couple lived below us. The Turkish couple had a little girl that would come and play with KaTilla all the time because they were the same age. Even though the little girl did not speak English, it did not stop them from playing. Children have their own language to communicate with one another. I would always say, let the Holy Spirit interpret between them.

When we first arrived in Germany, we were put on a waiting list for housing. This means that you live on economy outside of the military installation for no less than a year or two and wait until they call you. It was nerve-racking; I was not trying to wait that long, so I said a prayer. I said, "Lord, please move us to the top of the list and out of this place that we're in."

Then, in thirty days, we were at the top of the list. God heard me, thank You, Jesus! Now, we were on the Army post, and I was able to walk everywhere. I had three children at the time. My son was born in Germany and is the third child out of five. After settling down, we began to look for a church. The first one we went to was Presbyterian. At first, we did not know it was a Presbyterian service, but we went in, sat down, and we were up and out of the door in ten minutes. It was as quiet as a church mouse, which surprised me because, growing up, I knew that church was not supposed to be that quiet. It was not because we were Black; there were no "Amen," no nothing. Later, we found out that the chapel held a gospel service. So, we tried it, and we liked it; it was great. There were wonderful people. There was a lovely pastor and his wife with their children. The chaplain's wife had six children. We met others through the relationships that we developed there. Billy met with several men that would be at the church for prayer every week, and the invitation turned out to be more than what I could ever think. In 1991, I was at home when he walked in the door. At first, he did not say anything. Then he looked at me and said, "I just gave my life to the Lord."

I had no words for him; I had nothing to say. My face was blank, and I kept on doing what I was doing, which was cleaning the dining room. When Sunday came around, we were ready to go to church that morning and had such a great time that I gave my life to the Lord that very Sunday after Billy did the past weekend. Our lives were changed forever from that point on. One year after we had given our lives to the Lord, I received some news. To preface, I would go to the doctor for regular check-ups. If you have children, make sure to make it an important part of your life to go and get checked out. That day, I went to get a six-month pap smear. They took some tests that women get for this type of annual check-up—blood work and the works. After a little while had past, I began to wonder what was taking the doctor so long to get the test back to me. Then, I received a letter in the mail after about two to three weeks. I guess they wanted to make sure that the tests that were taken were correct. They had run the tests more than two times in fact. Unfortunately, everything was not ok.

When I read the letter that had come in the mail, it had said that I had been diagnosed with stage four cancer and that I needed to come in to see them right away. Of course, I waited a while before responding back to them. When I did, they wrote me off immediately; they told me that I had six months to a year to live. Currently, I was only twenty-three years old with my whole life ahead of me. I was a young mother with four children at this time. Very quickly, I made up my mind that I was going to live and did not care about what the doctor had told me. All I knew was that I was not going anywhere anytime soon. So, I tore the paper up and put it in the trash. When Billy came home, I told him. I do not remember what he said, and I did not ask him about how he felt at the time because I did not want him to worry about me. I then waited a good two months before I went and saw the doctor after he had been insisting that I come in as soon as possible. It was a God moment for me, and I did not want to hear anything negative. When Billy and I did go, it was as I had thought: all negative talking. The doctor then gave me choices to prolong my life, while I knew the only choice for me was God. So, I declined all of the options he offered. I even had to sign a waiver, saying that I refused all the treatments.

Later into the year, there were more tests that they'd wanted me to take. They were keeping an eye on me. With Billy in the military, they had to do wellness checks, and they really were not expecting me to last very long. Even still, I did everything they asked me to do. They needed to know the stages and progress that I was making or not making according to what they were thinking. I was all for it because whenever the time came that I was looking for, I needed them to know and have no explanation according to their own understanding. After all, God would get the glory out of this, and no doctor would take the credit for anything they could not explain. From the time I found out I had cancer, I set my face like flint. I was so focused, and there was no room for doubt to enter my mind, and there was no wavering in my thoughts. Through these difficult periods, you must drown out every negative thought that enters your mind. Instead, fill it with praise, worship, and the Word of God. I knew that God would work with me in threes, as He usually did.

When we were at our friend's house one evening, playing games, they called us for dinner. After we ate and it was time to go, we would always pray before leaving, especially if we had to travel a little way to get home. It would get intense when we would bow our heads in prayer. The Evangelist then began to step toward me and spoke to me. She described what the cancer in my body looked like; the shape and color of it. The Holy Spirit told her to get behind me and push against my stomach. So, I let her, and she pushed in three times. Immediately, I was sick to my stomach and ran to the trash can to vomit. It all came up. The cancer had left me, and I was healed at twenty-three years old.

It was uterine cancer that was spreading up through my stomach. Through the process of having it, I was in so much pain for three months. Even still, I did not give up. I knew believing in my healing was the only thing I could do. Just as Jesus looked at them (disciples) and said to them, "With men this is impossible, but with God all things are possible" (Mat. 19:26). It was possible that God would not have healed me, but since I did not give Him a choice, He had to. I had one more trip to the doctor, and there were more tests that I would have to take. The tests came back negative, and they were amazed. As a matter of fact, they were so amazed that it was news that spread throughout the military base. The chaplain on the base, that just so happened to be my pastor at the time, shared with us that people all over the base were talking about the lady that was healed of cancer. They called me "the miracle lady."

When they were congratulating me, I had no idea why until I had found out that everyone was looking at me as though I had walked on water or something. Our pastor and church family had been praying for me the whole time. I loved them so much and appreciated them and everything they did for me. I would be told that I would not have any more children when I was diagnosed with cancer after having my son in Aschaffenburg, and I then became pregnant and had my fourth baby in Frankford, Germany. Charrell was a unique child. I almost lost her to a blood clot in my uterus. At that time, when I went to the bathroom, something fell out of my womb. Later they would tell me it was a hematoma, but after it was out, I began hemorrhaging. The bleeding would not stop. I was rushed to the hospital by Billy, and I did not have to wait to be seen. They took me right in. It was a German hospital, and everyone spoke German with some English. It was a remarkably interesting experience. Thankfully, my baby was fine, and I was fine. She was carried full term. During the time I had uterine cancer, I was actually carrying her.

Now, I want to share something with you as you're reading. There is a difference between a medical healing and a miracle healing. Some people have been healed by medication, and they call it a miracle, but that is not so. You put your trust in man and medicine. So, medicine was your success, not God. What happened to me, I believe, was that I had divine healing. While we are alive, we have cancer cells in our body that are dormant. Mine were trying to become active once again. However, my body belongs to God, and I was bought with a price that was paid for me. I don't sin against my body, and I don't disturb the make-up of God's creation. Remember that God must fulfill His purpose through me and through you. The cancer cells cannot become active because God said so. If you do not agree, then you do not have to. That is okay. My faith carried me. I chose to believe in God, and He came through for me because that is the way it is supposed to be. We are not supposed to put our confidence in any man. "It is better to trust in the Lord: then to put confidence in man" (Ps. 118:8).

I am supposed to be taking high blood pressure medication, but I cannot take them. I had two choices: either take it or stop taking it and trust God. This was told to me directly by the Holy Spirit. I knew what my doctor was going to give me before he gave it to me. Most of the time, I can diagnose myself before I even get to the doctor's office. This is because we should know our body better than the doctor does. However, only some people do while others don't. They usually go into the doctor's office and come out with three or more prescriptions than they had before, not knowing that they got paid to write those prescriptions for you. So, I do not let my doctor give me anything. I usually ask about the side effects and many other questions. People, please ask questions instead of taking whatever the doctor gives you. When I went to the doctors, I started with one pill and then ended up with six. You take one and they give you more to combat the effects of another issue that one of the pills may cause. So, please be careful. There are more people in the Church on medication than there should be.

HAWAII

By the time we got to Hawaii, I was having a hard time adjusting. I had just spent three to four years in Germany, and now I had to move to Hawaii. Billy went ahead of myself and the children. While I was patiently waiting to hear for the word to come over, I was riddled with anxiety. It had been one of the places I had dreamed about going to see in my lifetime. Billy was there for a few months before we arrived, and he told me he would be looking for a church to go to before we got there. Later, he called me and told me he had found a church for us to go to. Weeks before we talked about a church to attend, I had a vision of a church. Before asking what it looked like, I had told him that I had a vision about the church we were supposed to be a part of and that this would be our church home. I told him the name of the street it was on, what the inside looked like, and what color the chairs were, along with the color of the carpet. I had just described to him the inside of the sanctuary when he let me know how amazed he was. I was right; everything I had just described was the church he had found. When I left Germany,

I found out that I was pregnant again. My Lord, it would be baby number five. So, then I decided that would be the last one, and I meant it. I had a conversation with God, I asked him if I could get a Tubal ligation, which is getting my tubs tied, God answered, yes. I believe that if I had gotten pregnant again, I would not have made it through the pregnancy. There were too many complications. My spirit spoke to me. You know when you get that feeling? I had that feeling.

My youngest baby girl, Deborah, was born in Hawaii. I asked the Lord what I should name her, and He told me "Deborah." I was to spell it the same way that Deborah was spelled in the Book of Judges in the Bible. However, Deborah didn't come into the world easily. When I went into labor with her, she was making her way to the end, and the doctor said stop pushing. I stopped, of course, and he looked and examined me, Deborah was coming feet first. So, he said they might have to do a c-section. I told him he wasn't and that I was having this baby natural. I was not giving the doctor any choice. I told him more than once that I was having this baby the normal way. The Doctor took me to another room, and I asked where we were going. Before I went, I had to have an epidural. So, I was in the room, and I was upside down when he stuck his whole hand in my womb and turned her around headfirst. Then they took me back into the delivery room, and I had my baby the natural way. The doctor had just proven to me that he'd had more than one option for me to have my baby normal. Deborah was a seven-pound baby girl and God's little prophet. We gave her over to the Lord. In fact, we gave all our children to the Lord.

After moving into our new home and getting acclimated to the place, I'd had the baby. After she was born, we had to move a couple of times, including when Billy got out of the military. He still worked on the base but with civilian personnel. We moved on to the economy, which was expensive with five children. It was a two bath, four-bedroom, one story home. At this time, we were a very young family. In my opinion, the rent was too high, so I asked God in prayer to knock off one hundred dollars from the rent price. Then the landlord arrived to get the rent for the second month, and this is what happened: They asked for one hundred dollars less for the rent. I thanked my Almighty God; I don't know if Billy knew about what I had done. After that happened, I asked myself, what would have happened if I had asked for more than one-hundred dollars? Yes, I did wonder this sometimes. However, there was no doubt in my mind that God would have honored what I asked for.

After being in our home for a while, I was cleaning one day Deborah was about three years old, and she began to sing. I noticed her singing became prophetic, so I just listened to her and the words she was singing since I had never heard them before. God was filling her mouth with prophetic songs. The song she was singing was a song of deliverance. During that time, I felt an unknown presence in the house as well. I had no idea what it was, but I just felt it was not right and the presence did not belong there.

It seemed that Deborah's songs were changing the atmosphere in our home, and whatever it was that was in the house had left. Our house had always been a safe place for anyone who would enjoy coming over and being our guest. As a young couple of twenty-four-year-olds, Billy and I did everything that we were told to do. At some point, I woke up and recognized what was happening to our family. Billy and I were at the church every

Sunday on time with our five children. We did not ever miss a beat once we got into a routine of what was expected of us. We had Bible study during the week and a Friday night service as most Black churches did. After a while of this routine, it began to take a toll on our children. Their teachers at school began to call me and say that they were falling asleep in class. Sometimes the teachers would let them sleep, sometimes they would not. I told Billy, of course, and at the time, his actions were uncertain. It was like he was just wanting to be obedient to service, but looking out for our children was our concern.

So, we agreed to cut down on church services, and I would stay home with the kids on Sunday nights. We did not go anywhere on school nights, which would put me in service twice a week because my family came first. Religion was telling us that we had to be in church every time the doors were open. We had to figure it out for ourselves not to put anything before our family.

There are some churches out there that have their believers thinking that they must be in church three to four times a week. The truth is you do not. Being in church four to five times a week will not get you any closer to God or Heaven. A relationship with and obedience to God will. It is the traditions of the old church that have taught people, and now it has become a learned behavior that we should be in the church building every time the doors open. There are those that are in retirement age that will not retire. I hear from God that he does not want me to retire yet. So, you don't retire from your position; you retire from the pulpit. The Church is not able to grow if you refuse to leave the pulpit. There is a generation that is being raised up to take their place. We are to teach them. The next generation have a work to do for their generation that God is raising them up for.

We have learned "religion," and this came from man not God. It's man that has come up with these ridiculous, man-made ideas. They don't receive teachings from the Word of God. They just have the teachings of man's ideas mixed with the truth. This is not every Church. I'm going to stop here on this subject.

FLORIDA

Finally, I was back home, stateside. That is just how I felt at the time. When we arrived at Homestead Air Force Base, we immediately began to look for a house, or at least, Billy did. I was with the kids, getting them settled in and ready to attend school, shopping for school clothes and school supplies. We stayed on the base in lodging during this time, and we were there for five months. There were eight of us in three rooms. Being so close in our room, Billy and I had some heart-to-heart talks. I laid in his lap one evening and cried while the kids were outside playing. Not knowing how to really start the conversation, I told him that he was not listening to what I was saying. He told me in return that I was not the one listening. Does this sound familiar to anyone? We went back and forth. However, we did not go to bed angry that night, but my heart was still heavy. I didn't know what to do, so I just went to sleep. Whenever I would get upset, I would always take a walk or go to Walmart late at night to just walk around and look at stuff. However, I never bought anything; it was to clear my head. It's not like the problem went away during these moments because it was still there. I still don't think we ever resolved the issue we had.

Soon I thought I would start looking for a job, and I found one very quickly at the AF lodge where we were staying. I found out they were hiring, so I went inquiring if the front desk position was available. The manager was in his office, so I knocked, and he said to come in. When I asked about the job, he told me to sit down and just began to interview me on the spot. Then I was hired. I think there was more going on with me than I had realized. I did not know what was going on with me or with us, but I would go outside and cry so much. I cried so hard that my head would start hurting, and then I would go to sleep. I would do this when Billy would go to work. At this point, we had been married for fourteen years. While we were in Florida, I met a lot of people while we were transitioning. In 2001, there was a gentleman that I met, and we became friends. Our relationship was simple, but there were times when there were longer conversations. Since I was married, I had boundaries set. Friends should have boundaries; it does not have to be with a guy, it can be with a girl too. I believe everyone should have them.

Anyway, one day I was off, and I went to the gentleman's hotel room where he was staying, which happened to be in the same lodging hotel we were staying at. I was in there for about forty-five minutes, not realizing how bad it looked. Even with how innocent it was, it still did not look good on my part. When I came out of the door, I saw Billy standing on the top of the ledge in the next building. Before I knew it, within a few seconds, he was standing in front of me. From this point of my life, my marriage and everything began to spiral out of control. I do not know what clicked in Billy's head, but there was something that happened to that man's brain. So, we all left the room and went to the office. He almost got me fired from my job while trying to get the man fired. However, I did not lose my job, and neither did the man, but there were questions that were asked, and they were answered. Since I was off the clock, I was not at risk of losing my job.

I was shaky for a couple of days because I could not believe what was happening. It got worse because Billy began to go places, he really had no business going and developing relationships that he would not normally have with men and women. When he asked me what happened in the room, I told him, but he did not believe me because he had already come to a conclusion on the matter. He thought that I had betrayed him; I am not ashamed because it *did* look that way. I had let my good be evil spoken of (Rom. 14:16). From that moment, he became an intentional destroyer because he was hurt. However, this did not cross my mind since my mind was somewhere else. You'd think he was reverting to what he'd learned in the military because his eyes were on a target, and I was it. That is when I realized it had hurt him to see me in a place where he thought I was not supposed to be because of how it looked. The thoughts that would come to his mind must have taken him somewhere he had never been before. From that point on, it seemed he was on a mission.

Later, I was at work when my co-worker asked me, "Charlotte, if I saw something I thought you should know, would you want to know?"

When I said yes, she said, "I saw Billy in a black car parked in a Wendy's parking lot."

I thanked her for telling me because I trusted her but had nothing else to say. Then another co-worker saw him at a Publix grocery store; he was not alone, and he sure was not with me. My so-worker happened to be standing behind him, and he did not recognize who she was at first. He carried on a conversation with the girl he was with, he said that he was lonely, and went on and on about what was going on at home. I guess he realized who my co-worker was later because after his conversation with the young lady, there was a surprise look on his face. I did not know why he was not acting like the person that I knew, and I could not comprehend what was going on because in my mind, I knew I had done nothing wrong.

Now, I'm not saying I was not somewhere where I was not supposed to be, because that part is true. I realize now that it looked terrible, and I put myself in a position to make him look at me in a different way.

Time passed, and he lost his job in Florida and had made the decision to move back to Hawaii, the place we had left. He returned to the same job that he had when we left because they had not filled the position yet. With everything that was going on between us, it was not good for him to leave and be alone. However, I was not leaving Florida since we had bought a house and the kids were in school. I already knew what it was going to be like with me not there with him, especially with the way he was acting in Florida. His behavior did continue, and more and more he would do crazy and stupid things. There was more damage he did, not only to me, but to himself, the kids, our friends, and everyone that was connected to us. They could not believe what was happening, even with not knowing the whole story. Everyone that had come from Hawaii to the mainland U.S. would have problems with their marriage. I did not understand it though. Extraordinarily few couples we knew during the time we were in Hawaii were still together.

One day, Billy went too far and became involved with a young lady. One evening, I was standing in my living room, vacuuming the carpet, when a feeling came over me of separation. The Holy Spirit had let me know Billy had taken his ring off his finger. There was an overwhelming feeling inside of me; my stomach was sick, and my heart dropped to my feet. I simply had nothing to say. I had thoughts going through my head a hundred miles an hour. While Billy was in Hawaii, God was showing me everything concerning him. I asked God, "Why?" I did not want to know what was going on with him. He would call me, and I would still talk to him, and he talked to the kids as well. While I had to take care of the kids, work, and pay a mortgage, he contributed $900 a month while the total was $1,168. So, I had to pay fully for school things for the kids, like clothes, utilities, and much more. I worked from three in the afternoon to eleven at night. I was now living a single parenting life, even though, legally, I was not single.

Later, Billy came home to visit while we were in Florida. This one time, he came home and had something to tell me. We had many conversations on the phone, so I do not know why he would choose to tell me while I was at work. He could have easily told me on the phone. He told me that the young lady he slept with was pregnant, even though I already knew because God had shown me a child. I was already prepared for the news because God was taking care of me. Even before this, God had told me the young lady's name. There was always something coming up with Billy, he chose to leave his family mentally and physically. When you have a disconnect from your spouse, you can see it naturally and feel it spiritually. A separation from my husband was like a separation from God. What was, was now no more.

He broke the order of our household, and since he did that, I felt lost. My communication with God was broken through the relationship he had with Him. To have a relationship with your spouse is to have a relationship with God. It is he who has the final say in the household, though he may consult you because he wants the wisdom you have to offer, not the self-offerings of your mind. He trusts you to give him what he seeks. The connection is more than a simple marriage. When your whole world becomes God, then you're right there with Him. "What therefore God hath joined together, let not man put asunder" (Mark 10:9).

For some reason, I was holding on to God deep in my heart. I was holding on and praying for something that I knew nothing about. I believed it was in my spirit. Even though my spirit knew, I did not think I knew it naturally. Then Billy left and went back to Hawaii, and I began a relationship with a guy that had been trying to talk to me for an exceptionally long time. I began to talk to him because the news Billy had just given me had broken me. I was alone now and didn't make enough money, so I went to see a lawyer about getting a divorce to see what I could do about child support and everything else that would be available to the kids and myself. However, it would not be enough for five children, so I said, "Forget it." It was like I was starting over again in the middle of my life.

Once I started to, there was a feeling of security and protection immediately. I had not gotten this from him in so long that I had opened a door that I could not shut on my own. The issue with Billy and me got worse. My dreams would prepare me for every conversation I would have with him on the phone. From my dreams, I knew everything, and not on purpose. Although I know this is not nice, I thought the young lady he was with had some mental issues. Why does it seem like when men leave their wives, they go after someone that is no better than the wife? I cannot remember how long he was in Hawaii, but we were separated for a while. While there, he went from the government civilian job to the Army Reserve, which meant that he had to go from Hawaii to Nebraska. The last time I saw him was when he came to pick up his car, and he took our son with him. This meant that I had the girls. We would have a few words that were not so pleasant, but when we would start having regular conversations, we did not curse one another out or anything. Being in two different mainland states, it felt a little strange to be apart like we were because we had been married for so long. It had been three years of not seeing him or my son. While talking on the phone, I would ask him questions like if he was seeing anyone, but, of course, I knew already. Everything that he was doing was not hidden; if he even thought I didn't know, I knew. I told him that I would not be coming to Nebraska if he was still doing the same things that he was doing in Florida. Instead, I was going to move back to Oklahoma where my family was.

NEBRASKA

After some time had passed and having conversation after conversation, I then moved to Nebraska. He had lied about everything, but I still took his word for truth and gave him the benefit of doubt. I wanted to trust him, so I moved to Nebraska where he was. It was clear that he wanted me there, but he also wanted to do whatever he wanted in my presence. One night, it had gotten really bad. He had asked me to go out with him on Friday, and I said yes. So, while I was waiting for him to come home from work, I was in the bathroom doing my hair when he walked in the room and looked at me with a strange look on his face. I ignored the look and asked him where we were going. He said, "I don't know where you are going, but I'm going out."

I looked at him with a blank face, and my heart sank into my stomach. I did not lose my mind, but I did want to lose it on him. I was so angry that I said to him, "All you had to say was that you didn't want to go!"

Then I went downstairs and sat on the sofa. Since it was Friday, the kids were on their way to the movies. So, I sat down and began to cry. We mentioned divorce that night for the second time. I then called my former pastor in Hawaii, and we talked for about two hours. He shared some things with me, and I shared some things with him. Everything Billy did, he did it to my face. You may ask why I stayed. I even asked God if I should, and He said it was my choice. I had well enough reason to divorce Billy. He did what he did on purpose, to hurt me even the more. I would not be wrong in what choice I made, but I did choose to stay. I asked myself the same question. Why would I choose to stay? We separated, he did what he continued to do, and I did what I wanted to do. He did become concerned and angry when he found out I was seeing someone. It was the same guy I had been seeing in Florida. I never changed guys because one was enough. I did not have time for all that. Things were already complicated, and the years with this guy saved my life. When I was with the other man, I would speak negative things into my life and contemplate suicide all the time. Then I would think about it and say, "But I can't, I have the kids to think about."

All the words coming out of my mouth always led back to, "I cannot not, because of my children." I fell into a state of depression, and I did not take any medication for it. All I did was work and come back home. The other man would tell me that I was better than most women he had ever seen in his life. I took care of my children, I took care of my house, and I took care of Billy, all while working a full-time job. I had a granddaughter as well at this point. Anyway, he told me things to build me up and not put me down. I never forgot about God, by the way. I still went to church, and then I would go home, cook, and cry myself to sleep. It was hard leaving the man I was seeing because he took care of my children and me. Even though I had developed feelings for him, I felt like it was an exchange taking place, like a prostitute taking money in exchange for sex. So, are you still wondering why I stayed? Me too! It was not love keeping me there with him. In fact, it had nothing to do with love. The thought of why I had to go through what I was going through had not entered my mind. It was my choice to stay. My good had been evil spoken of (Rom. 14:16). Being in a relationship with someone else for two years was not right. This was what was on my mind the whole time. I didn't try to justify my actions. I was hurting, and it was real; it was not going away.

There was a young lady, and she looked at me and said, "Charlotte, you are stronger than you think." What a way to find out how strong I was. Little did I know that it would be something to push me into my own strength. There was a lot I could have done to him and his job, but I did not do it. I had to make wise decisions concerning my children and myself. So, I took the easy way out and let another man do what God was supposed to do. He was willing to do it because he saw how hard I was working for our lives. This was a time I could have, and should have, sought the Lord. There were times that I did, and it seemed that when I did, that there was a sensation that nothing was going to come together. I cried for help, and I knew God heard me each time. All I did was cry when I went before Him.

I don't know if things ever calmed down, but we moved into another house together. After moving in a year later, Billy would get orders to go to Kansas. We talked about the kids staying where they were and finishing high school. When you're in the military and moving all the time, you want to be in one place permanently sooner or later. He met someone else while he was in Kansas. After spending two years in the house, I moved out into an apartment with the kids. Once again, he cut me off from our bank account. He did pay my rent at the apartment: $735, and that's it. Since our son was in college and we had one of our daughters in college, moving into a three-bedroom apartment was not so bad after all, considering what was taking place in my life. In the house we had been in, the rent was $1,300 plus utilities. At this time, my husband was an angry man. I was not making him make the decisions he was making for his life. I told him that he would dig a hole so deep that he would not be able to get out of it and that he was indulging in the hurt he was feeling.

Sin had taken over in his life because he gave himself over to it. Once you have crossed that line, it's hard to get back. You think differently, so your actions are different. What you would normally do, you don't do anymore. All the good things about your life become unimportant to you. Instead, your focus is on all the wrong because you're not comprehending that what you're doing is wrong. When you do something and it becomes intentional, you make progress, whether it's good or bad. You progress in it even if it's wrong.

During this time, Billy stayed away for a while. He would come visit the kids, but by this time, I did not care to see him anymore. One day, I went to the doctor because I was in so much pain. Later, I found out that my uterus was full of fibroids, so I had to see a specialist. Then my surgery was scheduled. However, while everything was already falling apart, so was the surgery. For a while, I thought it was okay—until I got out of the bed one evening. I stood up to go to the bathroom when I froze in midair. I could not move an inch. I had one foot in the bed and one foot on the floor. I could not move, and I could not even talk. My daughter came to my room and asked, "Mom, are you okay?"

How did she know to come to my room at that moment? I didn't know. When I tried to say her name, only my lips moved. The next thing I knew, she was standing right in front of me. She asked, "Do you want me to call an ambulance?"

All I could do was nod. The pain in my left leg was so overwhelming that no words would come out. I was rushed to the hospital instantly, and they began to prep me for emergency surgery. A small hole had developed in my ureter, and urine was running down the left inside of my leg. The doctor said it left lots of scar tissue, and the specialist that I was seeing did the emergency surgery. He put a stint in the ureter, which caused me to have to have a catheter. I was wearing a bag strapped to my leg, which would be emptied each time it got full. I had nine stints done, and each time, I had to be put under for surgery. My doctor sat me down and told me that I could not keep getting stints, and I was not healing fast enough. He saw it in my face that I was good with having to have surgery. I first had to gather myself together. I made it to the church parking lot before sitting there and crying uncontrollably.

Then I walked into the church to ask for prayer and left. At that moment, I was ok because I had finally calmed down. I ended up having major surgery. The doctor said he removed as much scar tissue as he could. Billy did show up but didn't stay for the surgery. When I woke up, I was in my hospital room, and my best friend, Jackie, was sitting in a chair. I was surprised to see her sitting there. When I looked toward my window, there were flowers sitting on the ledge. I asked who they were from before I read the card in the flowers. They were from Billy, and he wished me a happy life. Those flowers almost found themselves on the wall. It made me angry. *How stupid of you to get me flowers*, I thought. However, I did take them home.

Everything that I did not want to do, I found myself doing, which was strange to me. It had to be the Holy Spirit. He (the Holy Spirit) would make me think about my actions. Let me explain; have you ever been in a situation where you were on your way to tell someone off and when you got there, your words changed, the words were nothing you wanted to say, instead you spoke in a low controlled voice with more kind words than you were thinking in your head? That's what I'm talking about, so I took the flowers home. Jackie, a wonderful friend of mine, was sitting in the chair, talking and encouraging me, even when I was ready to give up. In my prayer and worship time with the Lord, I would only be travailing and interceding. I knew it was for Billy and not myself, though I needed prayer just as bad. Billy had told me many of the situations he was in, and at the time of every situation, I was on my knees. With the position I was in, I had to forget about myself and do what God wanted me to do when He needed it to be done. It was the hardest thing I had ever done in my life because we were not on good terms. What if you had to pray for someone who had walked all over you for seven years? Most would not have been able to do it. I didn't hate him. I couldn't hate him; I could not explain it. Going before God kept the bitterness where it belonged: out of my heart.

I was angry for a very long time. In fact, I was for years. My state of mind was not my own. The responses, reactions, and responsibilities, and the caring, loving, flexible person was still present. However, the Lord was everywhere. There was no time that His presence was not felt. I want to describe it to you, but there is no way that I can. It's like not having any food for ninety days and only drinking water; it was the Holy Spirit that made me strong. Everything was clear, I knew what I wanted and what I needed to do. When I was home from the hospital, there were families dropping off food, and the people I loved would visit. I appreciated every one of them for being there for my family. When Billy had come into town, I was up walking around and doing well. He then walked through the door and walked down the hallway just as I was exiting my room. He fell to his knees and began to speak in tongues. I stood, just looking as he wept. Looking at him, I asked "What is wrong?"

He looked into my eyes and told me that my countenance was like God. There was a gold, glowing light coming from my face. I said nothing. We sat down, and he talked to me. It was a very short conversation, and I told him to leave, and he left. I prayed and worshiped the rest of that day. God held me up once again as I began to pray for Billy after he left. I told the Lord that I would give up my marriage to save his soul. Billy would tell me that he did not know how to get out of what he was in, and before I knew it, he was calling me on the phone two weeks later, saying that he had military orders to leave Nebraska and go to Little Rock, Arkansas. I told him no and that someone better check it again. He then called me back and said that someone had reported to the position he was supposed to fill. Let me tell you, I was not feeling it. We were not going to Arkansas, and it was funny when I said it because I meant it. When he called me again, he said, "We're going to Texas."

I said, "Yes, we are."

AFTER TEXT

I pray that you liked what you read, and I know you have questions you would like to ask me. I can't imagine what's going through your mind as a woman. Questions like, "How did she do it? How did she handle the things that she had to go through? What was her go-to scripture to stand with and give her strength?" I was surprised as well. I will talk about all this in the revised version that I will be writing of this book. God told me to just get the story out, and I did. It took me a long time. I will share the process in which it took me to write such a short but powerful book soon. Blessings to all who have read it. May the love of God be with you, in Jesus's name.

SCRIPTURES

Psalm 18:1–2—King James Version

I will love thee, O Lord, my strength. 2 The Lord is my rock, and my fortress, and my deliverer; my God, my strength, in whom I will trust; my buckler, and the horn of my salvation, and my high tower.

Psalm 18:1–2—Message Bible

I love you, God-you make me strong. God is bedrock under my feet, the castle in which I live, my rescuing knight. My God-the high crag where I run for dear life, hiding behind the boulders, safe in the granite hideout.

Deuteronomy 20:4 King James Version

For the Lord your God is he that goeth with you, to fight for you against your enemies, to save you.

Deuteronomy 20:4 Message Bible

When you go to war against your enemy and see horses and chariots and soldiers far outnumbering you, do not recoil in fear of them; GOD, your God, who brought you up out of Egypt is with you. When the battle is about to begin, let the priest come forward and speak to the troops.

Isaiah 40:31 King James Version

But they that wait upon the LORD shall renew their strength; they shall mount up with wings as eagles; they shall run, and not be weary, and they shall walk, and not faint.

This verse is also translated as:

But those who trust in the Lord will find new strength. They will soar high on wings like eagles. They will run and not grow weary. They will walk and not faint.

Isaiah 40:31 Message Bible

But those who wait upon God get fresh strength. They run and don't get tired, they walk and don't lag behind.

Deuteronomy 31:6 King James Version

Be strong and of a good courage, fear not, nor be afraid of them: for the Lord thy God, he it is that doth go with thee; he will not fail thee, nor forsake thee

Deuteronomy 31:6 Message Bible

Be strong. Take courage. Don't be intimidated. Don't give them a second thought because GOD, your God, is striding ahead of you, He's right there with you. He won't let you down; he won't leave you.

1 Timothy 1:7 King James Version

For God hath not given us the spirit of fear; but of power, and of love, and of a sound mind.

1 Timothy 1:7 Message Bible

But God gave us a spirit not of fear but of power and love and self-control.

1 Chronicles 16:11 King James Version

Seek the Lord and his strength, seek his face continually.

1 Chronicles 16:11 Message Bible

Study God and his strength, seek his presence day and night.

Exodus 15:2 New International Version

The Lord is my strength and my defense; he has become my salvation. He is my God, and I will praise him, my father's God and I will exalt him.

Isaiah 41:10 Knew King James Version

Fear not, for I am, with you; But not dismayed, for I am your God. I will strengthen you, Yes, I will help you, I will uphold you with My righteous right hand.

Isaiah 41:10 Message Bible

Don't panic. I'm with you. There's no need to fear for I'm your God. I'll give you strength. I'll help you. I'll hold you steady, keep a firm grip on you.

Philippians 4:13 King James Version

I can do all things through Christ which strengtheneth me.

Philippians 4:13 Message Bible

Whatever I have, wherever I am, I can make it through anything in the One who makes me who I am.

Psalm 28:7 King James Version

The Lord is my strength and my shield; my heart trusted in him, and I am helped: therefore my heart greatly rejoiceth; and with my song will I praise him.

Psalm 28:7 Message Bible

Blessed be GOD- he heard me praying. He proved he's on my side; I've thrown my lot in with him. Now I'm jumping for joy, and shouting and singing my thanks to him.

www.ingramcontent.com/pod-product-compliance
Lightning Source LLC
Chambersburg PA
CBHW031236120626
46545CB00003B/1140